Being a Catholic

MICHAEL EVANS

CTS Publications

First published 1992 by the
Incorporated Catholic Truth Society
38–40 Eccleston Square
London SW1V 1PD

© 1992 The Incorporated Catholic Truth Society

ISBN 0 85183 853 7

Printed by The Ludo Press Ltd, London SW18 3DG

FOR A START

This booklet aims to give a very brief summary of the Catholic faith. What does the Catholic Church hold in common with the vast majority of Christians, and what is distinctive about its beliefs? This can be only a scanty glimpse of what is involved, and from but one of many possible angles, but I hope it will at least serve as a beginning, motivating you to read further and explore more deeply.

WE BELIEVE IN ONE GOD

The Christian believes in God, in one God. This does not just mean affirming that there is indeed a God. It involves placing our faith in him—really accepting him as my God, as your God, as our God, the Lord of our lives. It means refusing to worship the false gods of our day—power, pleasure, wealth—and instead trustfully yielding my whole life into his hands. It means saying and living a true 'yes' to his loving lordship, allowing his will of love to be done in me, and his Kingdom, his reign of love, to come about in my life.

PRAYER AND WORSHIP

Prayer is at the heart of a life open to God. Prayer is not about trying to change God's mind so that 'my will be done'. It is being aware of the presence of God who is with us always, opening ourselves to receive his free gift of himself and to be touched and transformed by the power of his love. It is abandoning ourselves completely to God with a deeper and deeper 'yes', not because of what we might get out of it, but simply because he is God and so that 'his will be done'.

In our prayer, we open our lives to the God who is always reaching out to us, giving himself to us. The deepest meaning of prayer is expressed in the first few lines of Psalm 62:

O God, you are my God, for you I long.
For you my soul is thirsting.
My body pines for you like a dry, weary land without water.

The heart of our prayer should be simply praise of God for his greatness and goodness, for the gentle majesty of his boundless love: it is right to give him thanks and praise, to lift up our hearts to the God who is the source of all we have and are. Prayer is also the time when we lift to him the needs of the world, coming into his presence with others in our minds and hearts. Such prayer of intercession is a powerful expression of our active love for others and of our trusting faith in God.

MAKER AND FATHER

Central to the whole Christian faith is that 'God is love' (I John 4:16). The Old Testament is full of powerful testimony to the wonder of that love. This reaches its climax in the New Testament message of the God who loves the world so much that he gives his only Son (John 3:16), the Son who lays down his life for us, his friends (John 15:13).

It was purely as a free gift of love that God made the universe. All that is not God, matter and spirit, seen and unseen (including the angels), is created by God. Whether he did this in six heavenly days or through billions of earthly years of evolution is not important. The Book of Genesis teaches that God is the creator of everything, and all he makes is good. Human beings are made in God's image and likeness (Genesis 1:26): we are personal, spiritual beings, able to love and be loved, and given a special dignity and responsibility by God himself (Psalm 8).

God is intimately involved with every moment of his creation from beginning to end, holding our lives in his hands and guiding us with fatherly care. We are totally dependent on him for every moment of our existence: in him we live, and move, and have our being. He is creator of the whole universe, but also my personal creator who 'knit me together in my mother's womb' (Psalm 139:13). He created my 'soul', the innermost 'me', able to love in response to God's eternal love. Because God is involved in our creation from the moment of conception, Catholics stress strongly the sacredness of human life from that first beginning.

God did not create things to exist in isolation, but in a harmony centred upon him, a harmony brilliantly expressed by the 'Garden of Eden'. God created us for deep communion of life with himself, with one another, and with the rest of creation. He continues throughout history his creative work of drawing us together into his life.

Jesus himself taught us to call God 'Father', the perfect parent who loves us with a perfect love. He is not just 'my Father' but 'our Father', the God who draws us together into his family as his own daughters and sons. Our deepest destiny is to share Jesus' own uniquely intimate relationship with his Father, able to use the affectionate term of address 'Abba' as Jesus did.

GOD REVEALS HIMSELF

God is so much greater than we can ever imagine! We know him because he reveals himself, opening his life and reaching out to us in many ways. We can catch glimpses of the Creator reflected in the wonders of his creation: the majesty of the universe, the splendour of many a landscape, the beauty of nature and especially our fellow human beings, made in God's image and likeness. We can see something of God in creation just as we can learn about great artists or composers from their masterpieces.

God shows himself in human history, especially in the story of the ancient people of Israel. He chose this small people to be 'a light to the nations', and made a special bond of friendship—or 'covenant'—with them. Through his constant presence, and in key events such as the great escape from slavery in Egypt (the Exodus), God gradually unveiled himself to his people while still remaining the Great Mystery, as he always will. The story of God's faithful love is recorded and interpreted in the Bible. This collection of books written over many hundreds of years is not just one more literary masterpiece. It is the word of God! Not only did God inspire the human writers in some mysterious way, but he continues to speak to us now through its words.

Christians see the Old Testament as reaching its climax in God revealing himself in Jesus Christ. The Bible moves from God's first creation in Genesis to the new creation which begins in Jesus, from prophets like Isaiah who spoke God's word to the Prophet who is God's Word in person, the Word made flesh (John 1:14).

The New Testament writings are the faithful witness of the first Christians to this Word, to Jesus of Nazareth. Jesus is God's revelation of himself in person as one of us, a fellow human being. The apostles were his chosen witnesses, and their faith in

Jesus is still the rock-like foundation of our faith today. This is why the New Testament is so fundamental to Christian life in every age: it is the Spirit-given record of the apostles' own handing on of the Good News.

The Spirit of Truth works in every Christian as he or she reflects upon God's word, but Catholic teaching stresses the role of the whole community, throughout the world and down through the ages, in faithfully interpreting the Scriptures, rather than just the isolated individual or any particular group.

The Church's doctrine does not change from generation to generation, but it does develop, much as the human being grows to maturity from its first beginnings in the mother's womb. The Christian community is called to explore ever more deeply the wonders of God's revelation. Ordained pastors (above all the bishops united with the Pope) have a special ministry of discerning which interpretations are really from God, keeping the Church's faith today firmly rooted in that of the apostles and of past generations. This idea of an authoritative teaching office *(magisterium)* is an important part of the Catholic way of seeing how God works in his Church.

SAYING 'NO' TO GOD

God freely offers us all that he has to give: the love that he is, the gift of himself, a share in his life.

But love is not something which can be imposed. God yearns for us to accept his gift, but we are left free to say 'No'. We cannot escape our total dependence on God for every moment of our existence, but we can refuse to respond to God's love. This is the core of sin: our free 'No' to God.

From our very beginnings, the human race has refused God's offer of intimate friendship. We have never become a truly Godly community, gathered together in him by his own creative love. However and whenever human life first appeared, from those first origins, we have preferred to place ourselves rather than God at the centre of our universe (original sin). The result is disharmony, with human beings at odds with God, each other and the rest of creation. Our real human freedom has been deeply wounded, though not totally destroyed. None of this takes away the goodness and blessedness of everything God has created.

There is no simple answer to the mystery of evil, especially the suffering of the innocent. This is something we all experience, challenging our faith in the God who holds all things in his hands. Evil deeds can be blamed on those who freely do such things. Suffering from natural disasters or diseases is often due to our blinkered perception of how nature works or our abuse of creation. Selfishness and greed have a deadly power to disrupt God's intended harmony for creation and to hinder our own ability to live harmoniously within that creation. In the end, the key to the mystery of suffering is the mystery of God himself, the God who personally plunged himself into the pain of the world on the cross.

In spite of being rejected by humanity, God has never abandoned us. Again and again God tried to draw his people back to himself; again and again he was rejected. God's love is unconditional, unchangingly boundless, reaching out to the sinner and sinful humanity in open welcome. Nothing in our past, present or future can make God abandon us.

THE SAVIOUR

God placed deep in the hopes of his people the promise of a saviour who would fulfil his plans for humanity. This was to be the Anointed One ('The Messiah' from the Hebrew, 'The Christ' from the Greek).

When the time was right, God sent this saviour, Jesus of Nazareth, born in humility and poverty of the virgin Mary (Luke 1:34–35). God began creation out of nothing by the power of the Spirit; now he began its renewal by creating the humanity of Jesus without a human father, once again by the power of the Spirit.

Jesus' active ministry began when he accepted baptism from John the Baptist (Mark 1:9–11). In this act of identifying with sinners, though sinless himself, Jesus' special-ness begins to be revealed: he is God's beloved son, anointed with his Spirit for the work of reconciliation.

Jesus began by proclaiming that God's reign, his Kingdom, was near at hand (Mark 1:15). The people were called to 'repent', to turn away from sin and come back to God. Jesus makes the same call to each of us, a call to real conversion, a change of heart, a spiritual revolution in our lives. We allow ourselves to be truly transformed by the overwhelming power of God's healing love, and welcomed into God's 'Eternal Life'.

Jesus was clearly an extraordinary person, revered today even by people who have no belief in God. But he was—and is—much more than that. Slowly but surely, Jesus unfolded what was unique about him, who he actually was.

He was aware of a uniquely intimate relationship with God, able to call him 'Abba', an affectionate term for one's father (Mark 14:36). He was conscious of having a unique authority, shown by the way he taught and his claim to divine powers, above all the authority to forgive sins (Mark 2:5).

Only after Jesus' resurrection were the full implications realized. Jesus was acknowledged as 'Lord', a word used of God by Jews of the time. Christians believe in Jesus as fully human and fully God. He is not just a marvellously good man in whom God worked, but a human being who is personally God: Jesus is God the Son in person, God-made-man, God's Word made flesh, 'true God from true God'. This belief is at the very heart of Christian faith: God himself, God the Son, has become a fellow human being, experiencing our life, suffering and death as 'God-with-us'.

THE CROSS

The cross is the key symbol of the Christian faith. This is rather strange when we consider its original meaning. Crucifixion was a humiliating and agonizing form of execution reserved for the lowest of the low in the Roman Empire—slaves, violent criminals and outcasts. The scourging, the hammering of nails through the wrists, the hanging naked in a public place, all made crucifixion an especially horrific and scandalous death. It is hardly surprising that both Jews and Gentiles mocked when Christians claimed that this crucified preacher was Lord and Saviour of the world (I Corinthians 1:23).

This is the depth to which God was prepared to descend for our salvation (Philippians 2:8). Not only did God's Son experience death with us, but he suffered what was commonly held to be the most scandalous of deaths, the death of an outcast. In the cross of Jesus, God plunged himself to the very bottom of the pit of human life.

The Lord of the universe does not stand aloof from suffering. God immersed himself personally into the disharmony which had come to creation, experiencing it in all its pain so that he could bring healing and renewal from within. Jesus himself is the supreme instance of totally innocent suffering. When we turn to Jesus in our suffering or that of others, we turn to the God who knows our pain from the inside. On the cross God became totally 'at one' with us so that the division between us and him could be overcome. It is through his wounds that we are healed (Isaiah 53:5). By sharing human life and death, Jesus removed their godlessness and put God back into both of them.

The cross reveals starkly the greatness of God's love even in our sinfulness (Romans 5:7–8). If you want to know what God is really like, look at the cross—it tells more of God than any words!

HE IS RISEN!

Easter is the greatest festival of the Christian year, a feast full of the promise of new life.

God the Son descended to the very bottom of the pit of human life on the cross, but he went so low in order to lift us out of that pit into new and eternal life. God the Father raised his Son Jesus from death, not back to an earthly life like Lazarus, but to a new and glorified life. The apostles and others really experienced the risen Jesus, but in a mysterious way, recognizing him with the eyes of faith (Acts 3:15). Jesus is still our fellow human being, but one whose life has been transfigured and transformed.

Christians are the Easter People! We look forward with boundless hope to being raised with Jesus after death (John 11:25–26), but Jesus is with us, and we can become truly alive with his risen life here and now if we accept him as Lord and open ourselves to him. Jesus' resurrection can be our resurrection if we allow our old self to be put to death and let the Lord raise us up with him (Romans 6:1–11). Dying and rising with Jesus is central to Christian living, reaching its climax at death itself. Now that God has gone through human death in Jesus, death can be the final step of our pilgrim journey into the heart of the living God. Jesus' death is the death of our death: dying he destroyed our death, rising he restored our life.

The life, death and resurrection of Jesus was the central event in human history, the turning-point for all creation. Human life and death has been broken open and transformed by the wonder of Easter, and the new creation has begun.

AT-ONE-MENT

Jesus saved us by his death and resurrection. 'Salvation' is a word we often use, but what does it really mean to be 'saved'?

Christians over the centuries have looked at salvation from many different angles: Jesus triumphed over Satan, death and sin, setting us free from evil of every kind; by his death and resurrection he has taken the sting out of death and made possible new and eternal life for each of us; he has taken our sins upon himself, offering to the Father the loving and free sacrifice of his death as 'satisfaction' for those sins; he reveals to us the overwhelming love and mercy of God, enabling and inspiring us to live the way of holiness.

Behind all these ideas is that of atonement. Although it has come to mean primarily making amends for wrong-doing, the fundamental meaning of the word is that of reconciliation, at-one-ment, putting 'at one' those who were estranged. By Jesus' death and resurrection, we are claimed back by God ('redeemed') and a healing wholeness is bestowed on us ('salvation'). The heart of everything is our reconciliation with God, a free gift which fills us with joyful trust (Romans 5:11). We are made whole by being drawn into that deep and intimate relationship with God for which we were created. Because Jesus unites in himself God and humanity, both are made truly 'at one' in him, and an incredible communion between God and us is made possible, already now in this life and in fullness in heaven.

Our at-one-ment with God is far more intimate than we can imagine. We become living temples of God's presence: 'the love of God has been poured into our hearts by the Holy Spirit which has been given us' (Romans 5:5). It is the Spirit who brings about our deep communion with God, so that God lives in us and we in God (see chapter 4 of St John's first letter).

God wills everyone to be saved, but Jesus is the only saviour (I Timothy 2:4–6), the only human being who is personally God. We are not saved by what we do, but by Jesus drawing us into his Father's life. Salvation is not limited, however, to those who reach an explicit faith in Jesus here on earth. The risen Jesus is present to every human being, and people may be united to him in love even when they fail to recognize him (Matthew 25:31f.). God's saving grace is at work in all people of good will, and we leave their 'at-one-ment' to the hidden workings of the risen Lord, reaching out to the world through his Church.

Our at-one-ment is not just about personal reconciliation and communion with God. Being gathered together with each other in harmony and love as one people, one family, is a vital aspect of Jesus' saving work. Communion with each other goes hand in hand with communion with God. Salvation involves therefore the destruction of all barriers between human beings, and the formation of a real community centred around Jesus himself. Being saved is a truly family affair! Anything that undermines human unity—unjust sharing of the world's resources, discrimination, torture, the violation of human rights—must be worked against in the name of Jesus so that his victory over the Evil One and sin can be completed. The Good News of God's Kingdom includes liberation from everything that oppresses us, including poverty and injustice. God sets us free to love and be loved, and to share his life together as brothers and sisters in one family.

Although it has deep implications for our lives here and now, there is infinitely more to 'salvation' than simply creating a better world. Some of the richness of this mystery is proclaimed at the Easter Vigil:

> The power of this holy night
> dispels all evil, washes guilt away,
> restores lost innocence, brings mourners joy;
> it casts out hatred, brings us peace,
> and humbles earthly pride.
> Night truly blessed when heaven is wedded to earth
> and humanity is reconciled with God.

THE HOLY TRINITY

Being saved means being welcomed deep into the life of God. This is possible only because of the kind of God he is—the Holy Trinity.

We believe in only one God, yet we believe the Father is this one God, his Son is also this one God, and the Holy Spirit, poured out by Father and Son together, is this one single God. Three really distinct persons–Father, Son and Holy Spirit–who are each equally and perfectly all that it means to be God!

We can never come anywhere near fully understanding the wonder of the Trinity. It is the great mystery of the living God. But we can grasp something of the vital importance of this doctrine for us.

The doctrine of the Trinity tells of the God who is boundlessly loving and generous. Real love always involves giving oneself, sharing oneself, the joyful sacrifice of all one has and is. God the Father **is** love! He pours out his whole being in selfless love, and this total giving of himself **is** his Son, his Word who became flesh. God the Father and God the Son as one pour out their being in mutual love, and this total giving **is** the Holy Spirit, God's breath of living love.

This is not something which happened in God's life 'once-upon-a-time': it is how God is eternally, a totally selfless, generous, self-giving and loving God who is so rich in love that he is never emptied, the God who is very much active and alive. This is the wonder of the Trinity!

It is because the Father eternally pours out his Son that he can send him to share our lives as one of us. Father and Son together share with us the power of their mutual love, the Spirit of their life.

God reaches out to each of us, seeking to live within us and for us to live deep within him. This is what we mean by grace: God giving himself to us. If we say 'Yes' to this gift, opening our lives to Jesus and the Spirit, then marvellous things happen. We are changed deep within ourselves and become truly holy, radiating the presence of God within us. For all our weakness, we may well find that God speaks through us to others and touches their lives in many wonderful ways.

We cannot save ourselves; only God can do that for us. If we say a 'Yes' of living faith, and really live our response, we do so only because God himself is with us, opening us up to himself by the power of his love. It is always God who loves us first and makes the first move towards us (I John 4:19).

SAYING 'YES' TO JESUS

Jesus asked his disciples: 'Who do you say that I am?' (Matthew 16:15). He asks each of us the same question. If my answer is that he is indeed 'the Christ, the Son of the living God', then my whole life will be centred on him as 'My Lord and my God' (John 20:28). I will freely accept his lordship over all that I am, all that I have and all that I do–my way of life, my relationships, plans and hopes.

The risen Lord is standing at your door now, knocking and waiting for you to open your life and invite him in (Revelation 3:20). The decision is yours!

Know that he will come if you invite him. He promises: 'Ask and you will receive, seek and you will find, knock and the door will be opened to you' (Luke 11:9). He will come because he is already there, giving himself to you and loving you before you even think to ask. You will not necessarily feel his presence. Sometimes you will know a deep peace and joy, at other times you will feel nothing. That does not mean he is not there. Our faith is built upon his promise, not on how we feel.

We are called to believe with all our heart that Jesus is the Son of God. This is not just giving our mind's assent to the truth about him. It means a total turning of our life towards Jesus, real conversion. This involves turning away from sinfulness; otherwise our life will not be truly open to his presence. We put our trust in him, and make him the centre of our lives, becoming his disciples.

There is a second question Jesus asks: 'Do you love me?' (John 21:15). Love is the heart of a living faith, and of the whole Christian life. We are each called to a deep personal friendship with the Master who calls us friends (see St John's Gospel chapter 15 for a powerful expression of the meaning of discipleship).

The call to discipleship involves a daily challenge to deeper conversion, even if we experience especially powerful moments of opening our life to the Lord. Each day, the risen Jesus calls you by name and comes to your life, asking you: 'Do you believe in me?' and 'Do you love me?' Each day he lays his hands upon you and gives the strength of his love so that you can answer with an ever deeper 'Yes' by the way you live.

Personal prayer each day is vital. It gives the silence we need to hear the Lord as he calls us and touches our lives, filling us with the Spirit of his love. In the silence we can put our faith in him afresh, renewing our commitment to him and saying with St Peter, 'Lord, you know that I love you.' In such prayer the Lord becomes more truly the centre of our lives, and our hearts are transformed more deeply by his presence within us.

LIVING OUR 'YES' TO THE LORD

Being a Christian involves living the Way of Christ rather than the ways of the world. Our 'Yes' of faith to God's free gift of salvation has to be embodied in how we live. It is nonsense to call Jesus 'Lord' unless we actually accept his lordship over every aspect of our lives.

Jesus tells us to show our love for him by keeping his commandments (John 14:15). This means the Ten Commandments (really a Rule of Love), especially in the richly positive way taught by Jesus, and above all Jesus' own great commandment: loving God with our whole being, and loving others as Jesus loves us (Matthew 22:37–40; John 15:12).

Jesus did not lay down guidelines for every aspect of Christian living, but he did give us the basic principles. Our personal conscience is a vital way in which the Lord guides us, but conscience is not merely a feeling about whether something is right or not. It involves being really open to what God is saying to us, through his laws written into creation, through the Scriptures and through the community of faith and its authoritative leaders.

The way of a disciple is not an easy one. It is much easier to do as I please, to set myself up as my own personal authority, the lord and centre of my life. Discipleship means saying 'No' to much that the world regards as normal and acceptable. Jesus calls his disciples to renounce themselves, take up their cross every day and follow him (Luke 9:23). The sorrows, difficulties, pains and tragedies of life will still be there, but the Christian lives full of hope in the promise of life in abundance.

Discipleship, however, does not mean a life of misery and puritanical boredom. God has given us the world as a blessing. All creation is good and there for our joy: this includes the beauty of nature, the gifts and talents of one another, our own bodies including our sexuality, and our families, friendships and relationships. Only if centred on their Creator and used in accordance with his will of love will they bring deep and lasting happiness. Only God himself can really fill and satisfy our hearts.

We are all called each in our own way to be a living example of the wonder of being a Christian, a living sign that Jesus is truly risen and alive within us.

THE COMMUNITY OF DISCIPLES

Some people see being a Christian as simply a matter of a personal, even private, relationship between the Lord and each individual. The New Testament makes it clear that there is no such thing as a purely individual Christian faith, avoiding belonging to the Church, the community of disciples.

Jesus came to bring about a new 'at-one-ment' or communion between God and his people. Jesus formed his disciples into a group closely united around himself, and the same is true of his disciples today. Unity with one another is central to being saved by Jesus. Faith in Jesus and discipleship of him are communal by their very nature. We are members of God's one family, and so brothers and sisters of each other. The New Testament describes Christians as members making up the one body of Christ, living stones built together into a dwelling-place for God (Romans 12:4–5; I Peter 2:5). I can no more be a 'Churchless' Christian than a part of the human body can survive cut off from the rest. The Holy Spirit dwells in each of us, uniting us with Christ and with one another in an intimate communion of lives.

Christians gather together into communities which worship and live their Christian faith together. This visible unity is an important part of being a Christian. These local gatherings are not simply human communities like any other. God himself is deeply involved, making us the People of God the Father, the Body of Jesus Christ, the living Temple of the Holy Spirit. A community of disciples is most fully a true 'church' of Christ when it gathers together to celebrate the Eucharist, listening to God's word, entering deeply into Jesus' offering of himself, and receiving his 'at-one-ing' presence in Holy Communion.

Local eucharistic communities (parishes, etc.) are led by one or more ordained ministers (priests and deacons) as living signs of the risen Lord. Every Christian is called to serve the local community of disciples in his or her particular way. All members of a church need each other and depend on each other, and we each have special gifts from God for building up the church in its work for Christ (I Corinthians 12). All of us together are that Church.

THE CATHOLIC CHURCH

As an individual Christian cannot be a full disciple without belonging to a community of disciples, so also a local church cannot be truly a church on its own, in isolation from other Christian communities.

The local church belongs to a community of such churches called a diocese, gathered round their bishop. The bishop serves the unity in faith of all the communities in his care, keeping them faithful to the teaching and mission of the apostles. Bishops are in a real sense successors of the apostles, carrying on their authoritative witness to the risen Jesus and their pastoral care of the churches.

Once again, even a diocese cannot be fully a 'church' in isolation, but only if it is in communion with the worldwide community of churches, the universal Church of Christ.

In Catholic teaching, the Bishop of Rome, the Pope, has a central role in preserving and deepening unity among all the bishops of the world. Each diocese shows its communion with all the others by linking itself visibly in faith to Rome and its bishop.

Peter was given a special role by Jesus, to be the 'rock' on which the Church was founded, the central foundation stone among the twelve apostles. He was to strengthen his brothers, preserve their unity, and feed the flock of Christ (Luke 22:32; John 21:15–19; Matthew 16:15–19). Catholics believe that the Pope is a successor of St

Peter, continuing his ministry of being chief shepherd among his fellow shepherds, always as the servant of Christ himself, the Good Shepherd. This is the purpose of the primacy of the Pope, a primacy of love.

Authority in the Church, understood by Jesus in terms of service, is exercised above all by the bishops of the world united with the Pope. Sometimes they gather in great councils like the Second Vatican Council in the early 1960s which met to renew the Church for its mission in the modern world. Sometimes the Pope speaks as chief pastor to the whole Church.

In Catholic teaching the Holy Spirit works through the bishops as instruments in keeping the Church today faithful to Jesus and to the apostles' witness. Because it is so important for God's people not to stray from the truth of Christ, we believe that when the bishops together speak with authority to the whole Church on a matter of faith or morals, the Spirit preserves them from error. This is also true of the Pope if he speaks with his full authority as chief pastor. This is what Catholics mean by an infallible teaching office. It does not mean that every time the Pope or bishops say something, they must be right; it only applies under certain strict circumstances when an authoritative statement is needed. When divisions on doctrine threaten the Church's unity in faith, it is vital that there should be an effective ministry which can faithfully discern what teaching is truly from the Lord. It is really God's own way in a human community of keeping his promise to remain with his disciples and to keep them faithful to himself.

CATHOLICS AND OTHER CHRISTIANS

The Church is a 'communion', a community bound together by what we hold 'in common'. The more we share, the more 'in communion' we are with each other. Catholics believe that certain key visible elements are willed by Jesus for his Church. These include the New Testament and its faithful interpretation; all seven sacraments; the ministry of bishops, priests and deacons, and the ministry of the Pope, all serving the visible worldwide communion of the Church; also the whole Tradition of the Church through the ages, a living communion with the faith of the great Councils of the Church and of the saints, so that we believe now what they believed then.

Only Christian communities which have 'in common' all of these key visible elements share 'full communion'. The Catholic Church sees itself as being unique in having this fullness of visible communion. Others have 'partial communion' in varying degrees depending on how much they share. This says nothing about Christians' commitment to Christ, holiness of life or zeal for the Gospel.

Every Christian and Christian community throughout the world should be fully visibly united as a powerful sign of the 'at-one-ment' Christ came to bring. Tragically, divisions have occurred over the centuries. The Eastern Orthodox Churches share almost everything in common with Catholics, but there are difficulties to overcome before full reunion is possible. Protestants in the West abandoned communion with the Pope and re-interpreted the Church's faith in ways unacceptable to the Catholic Tradition. Faults lay on both sides, and serious efforts are being made to heal the divisions. The Catholic Church is totally committed to this work of reconciliation. Tremendous progress has been made in recent years, and we now understand each other much better, working and worshipping together more closely. This movement towards Christian unity ('ecumenism') does not mean abandoning or watering down our Catholic faith. It does however involve being prepared to listen and to learn from others, to rediscover our common heritage, and to enrich our tradition with the insights of other Christian communities.

PROCLAIM THE GOOD NEWS

The whole Church, the worldwide communion of local churches, is the People of God, the Body and Bride of Jesus Christ, and the living Temple of the Holy Spirit. It is a community with a mission, or rather, the community through which the Lord continues his own mission of saving the world.

Proclaiming the Good News ('evangelization') is the deepest identity of the Church. We are all called to announce and to live the Good News of Jesus, to be together a community which is the living Gospel for all to hear. Every Christian is a missionary, set aside to bring Jesus into the lives of others. This is true no matter what kind of life we lead. Lay people have the special call to bring the presence of Christ into the everyday life of the world.

The Good News is about the salvation of the whole person and of every person, not just 'saving souls' but saving the human community. The Church has to be involved in setting people free not only from sin, but also the consequences of sin such as poverty and oppression. Popes and gatherings of bishops this century have stressed again and again that action for justice and human rights is something at the very heart of proclaiming and living the Gospel message.

We believe that the Church is one, holy, catholic and apostolic. These marks are gifts from God to his people, but they are also tasks. The Church is already one, but Christians must grow ever closer in God's love so that they can be visibly united. The Church is already holy, but needs to be continually purified and renewed until it reaches perfection in heaven. The Church is already catholic and universal, but it must be even more open and welcoming, reaching out in Christ's name to every human being. The Church is already apostolic, but it is called to become ever more faithful to the faith and mission of the apostles. Christ's Church is already a worshipping and witnessing community, but we are always challenged to share more actively in all that it is and does.

SACRAMENT

At the very heart of Catholic Christianity is the idea that God gives himself to us through human signs and gestures. God works mysteriously and invisibly, but in a way suited to us as human beings. Sacraments are about meeting God in a truly human way.

We use signs and symbols all the time to express our inner selves to others, making the invisible (love, for example) present through something visible (a card or letter, some words, a gift, a touch). This is the natural human way of communicating, rooted in how God himself created us, and it is the way God freely chooses to give himself to us: the invisible through the visible. The Catholic faith makes no sense without this central idea.

Signs range from 'mere signs' which point to something somewhere else, to deeper and richer signs which somehow make present what they signify (the gift which makes your love present to another, the hug or kiss which 'embodies' your invisible feelings). A sacrament is the deepest and richest kind of sign, one which actually 'contains' and 'confers' what it points to—the living presence of God himself. The Lord is present immediately, personally, 'face-to-face', but in a human way, through something visible.

Jesus is **the** sacrament, the visible presence of God in the world, the unique human way in which God speaks to us and gives himself to us.

As Risen Lord, Jesus is no longer visible. His Church is the living sign or icon of his saving presence in the world. It is through our involvement in its life that we meet Jesus and are drawn closer to him. We together are this sacrament, and our common life is meant to be the visible sign of Christ's invisible presence. This is the great mission of the Church: to be the 'universal sacrament of salvation', the living communal sign and instrument to all the world of Christ's saving, 'at-one-ing' work. The Catholic faith is that the Church is not just a fellowship of believers and worshippers, but a community through which the Lord reaches out to the world.

We ourselves need the Lord's presence. Through the seven sacraments, Jesus guarantees his powerful transforming presence at the crucial moments of our Christian lives. They do not limit the Lord, but they are central, visible ways in which he acts. A sacrament is about Jesus touching us in a very personal way, through the Church which is his Body. As in any relationship, such signs do not work like magic. Jesus promises his active presence, but we have to respond with faith and love.

THE RITES OF CHRISTIAN INITIATION

The Lord's drawing us into the deepest mysteries of his life is the greatest thing that can happen to us. The Church therefore treats its rites of welcome or initiation with great seriousness, challenging both the new disciple and the Christian community to reflect deeply on their meaning. When an unbaptized adult asks to join the Church, there is a formal process which includes acceptance by the Bishop, instruction and prayer, a gradual welcome into the life of a local church community, and finally the three sacraments of initiation (Baptism, Confirmation and Eucharist), received together at one great celebration, ideally the Easter Vigil. For a young child, the path of initiation is a journey over several years, but the meaning is the same.

BAPTISM

John the Baptist pointed away from himself to Jesus, the Baptizer. The word 'baptize' comes from the Greek for 'to dip', 'to immerse', 'to plunge'. John plunged people into the water of the river Jordan; Jesus plunges us into the Living Water of the Holy Spirit, immersing us deep into the life of God.

It is in the sacrament of Baptism that the individual meets Jesus the Baptizer. The community of the Church is central to the meaning of Baptism. It is through being plunged into the Church that we are plunged by Jesus into his life with the Father in the Spirit.

Water is something rich in symbolism. We tend to take it for granted, but in the Middle East water is the great symbol of life, used for cleansing, refreshing, bringing life and growth. The priest or deacon pours water three times over the person's head, saying 'I baptize you in the name of the Father and of the Son and of the Holy Spirit.' Through this pouring, God pours out the cleansing, refreshing and life-giving water of his Spirit.

Baptism in the early Church was by total immersion, bringing out much more clearly the deepest meaning of the sacrament: not just being washed clean of sin, but being plunged deep into the life of the Trinity.

In Baptism, God overcomes the great gulf between us and him brought about by humanity from its first beginnings ('original sin'). He adopts us as his beloved sons and daughters, making us members of his family. Jesus tells us that we must be 'born again' of water and the Holy Spirit (John 3:3–8). We emerge new-born from the baptismal water to begin our new life with God. This may well come alive for us later in life, but it is at our Baptism that this new birth takes place.

Baptism involves 'dying and rising with Christ' (Romans 6:1–4). We die to sin, freed from all past sinfulness, and rise to share the joyful power of Easter.

By Baptism we are made living parts of the Body of Christ, the Church. We together are Christ's Church, a community intimately united with the living Jesus, and so sharing his royal dignity, his priestly office and his mission to the world. The Holy Spirit is poured into our hearts, uniting us to Jesus and to each other 'in him'. Baptism unites us visibly with every other baptized Christian, the foundation of our search for deeper unity together.

Baptism is the beginning of a life of pilgrimage. The Israelites escaped from slavery through the waters of the 'Red Sea'; the baptized person escapes from slavery to sin through the waters of Baptism, and begins a life-long journey to the Promised Land of eternal life with God. We need to say a deeper and deeper 'Yes' to all that our Baptism means, and live every moment of our lives 'baptized in the Spirit', plunged deep in the life of God.

Infant Baptism is common practice among Catholics. Being an infant does not make a child unable to receive love or to belong to a family, whether of his or her parents or of God. Jesus loved children and welcomed them, and there has been infant baptism in the Church since its earliest days. Sacraments are God's key visible way of continuing his saving work, and Baptism ensures the infant's salvation. The salvation of those unbaptized is left in the loving hands of our Father.

CONFIRMATION

In the early Church, the rite of Baptism was completed by a public anointing by the Bishop. This developed into the distinct sacrament of Confirmation.

We can compare Confirmation with two events in the New Testament. Firstly, Jesus' baptism by John, which was more like a 'confirmation'; he was already God's Son and servant, filled with the Spirit, but now he receives a special giving of the Spirit and begins his public ministry as Messiah and Saviour (Luke 3:21–22). Secondly, the Pentecost experience of the apostles; they were already disciples of Jesus, but now they are strengthened by the Spirit to go out into the world and proclaim the Good News (Acts 2:1–13).

At our confirmation, we are drawn deeper into the whole meaning of the Church, which is not just a worshipping fellowship but a community sent forth by Christ. In confirmation Jesus commissions you personally to be a living witness to him in the world.

The person being confirmed is anointed with the oil of chrism, usually by the Bishop, who says: 'Be sealed with the gift of the Holy Spirit.' The sacrament is a new outpouring of the Holy Spirit, consecrating and officially commissioning us as full members of the Church. Such a task requires strength and courage. This is why we need our personal Pentecost. The Spirit does not come to us as a mighty wind or as tongues of fire, but he does come with the same gently strengthening and transforming power which banishes fear and sends us out full of faith to proclaim the Lord, with special gifts for the service of Christ in his Church.

Jesus says to the confirmed Christian: 'As the Father sent me, so am I sending you' (John 20:21), and 'Be my witness throughout the world' (Acts 1:8).

THE EUCHARIST

At the heart of the life of every real Catholic is the celebration of the Eucharist, the Mass, which Jesus told us to do in memory of him.

Every year, Jews celebrate the Passover, the beginning of their rescue from slavery in Egypt. They eat a special meal, including unleavened bread and cups of wine, and in Jesus' time the whole meal was centred on eating a lamb sacrificed the day before. They remember what God has done for them, and that great event comes alive so they can share in its fruits: the new friendship between God and his people (the 'Covenant'), and the freedom God achieved for them.

Before his arrest, Jesus ate the Passover meal with his disciples, but transformed its meaning as he did so, from a meal celebrating liberation from Egypt to one celebrating the liberation from sin and death which he was to achieve by his death on the cross. He himself was to be the sacrificed Passover lamb shared by God's people.

Jesus took the bread, and identified it with himself: 'This is my body which will be given for you' (Luke 22:19). After they had eaten the lamb together, he took the cup of wine and identified that with himself as well: 'This is my blood, the blood of the covenant, which is to be poured out for many' (Matthew 26:28). Jesus was saying, 'This is me, giving myself for you.' Catholics believe that Jesus meant what he said, and that this is still true today when we do the same in memory of him. When we eat the bread, and drink from the chalice, it is the Lord himself we receive. This is because Jesus actually changes the deepest reality of the bread and wine (their 'substance'), regardless of how they appear, into his own Body and Blood. By the power of the Spirit, they become the 'Blessed Sacrament' of the Lord's body given for us, his blood shed for us.

There is much more to the Eucharist than reading the Scriptures, saying prayers and receiving the Lord's presence in Holy Communion. It is Jesus' body given for us and his blood shed for us that is present, in other words Jesus sacrificing himself for our salvation. By taking part in this celebration, we are made 'at one' with Jesus in his once-for-all sacrifice.

The Eucharist is the greatest act of worship we can give to the Father. We are not worshipping on our own, trying to reach God of our own accord, but in deep communion with Jesus in his worship, his total giving of himself.

The Eucharist is the sacrament of salvation: all that Jesus has achieved for us by his death and resurrection is made present under the visible signs of the Church's worship in memory of him. Christ's sacrifice is not repeated, but the deepest mystery of Calvary and Easter is made present for us, so that we can be drawn into it and share it in full. Through the Mass, we enter into the movement of Jesus' self-offering, his loving sacrifice. The offering of our own lives as the Body of Christ is taken up by the Lord and united to his own offering as Head of the Body. As a community united with Christ, we are taken up 'through him, with him and in him' into the heart of God, and become ourselves an everlasting gift to God. We celebrate not only on our own behalf, but for the whole human race, living and dead, allowing the mystery of Calvary and Easter to radiate powerfully into the world around us.

All this is what we mean by the Mass being a sacrifice. It is the presence among us of the risen Lord and his whole saving work, and there is no greater thing we can do on earth. This is why the Catholic Church insists so strongly that we celebrate Mass at least every Sunday and Holy Day. Sunday in particular is the Lord's Day, the day set aside to worship him, and the day when Jesus rose from the dead. There is no better way of worshipping and celebrating than coming together to share in the Eucharist.

As each of us receives the Body and Blood of Jesus, we are drawn closer to each other, and the bonds of communion between us are deepened and strengthened. We are a people across the world who hold 'in common' the full presence of Jesus himself and a union in faith with his saving work.

Although the Eucharist deepens our unity, Catholic teaching sees receiving Holy Communion as the sign of the full visible communion we already share. This means that normally we cannot share sacramental communion with Christians who are not in full communion with us. The pain we feel at this reflects the pain of our division, and should urge us to work for full Christian unity so that we can share the Eucharist as truly one.

Once Mass is ended, we continue to treat any 'bread' left over with reverence as the 'Blessed Sacrament' of Christ's presence. It is kept in the tabernacle, and from this 'reserved sacrament' Holy Communion is taken to the sick. Sometimes it is placed on the altar as a focus for our adoration of the Lord, the sacrament of the fullness of his presence.

As the Israelites were given 'bread from heaven' or manna by God on their journey to the Promised Land, so Jesus gives himself to us as the new manna, 'the bread of life', real food and real drink for our pilgrim journey to God (see St John's Gospel chapter 6 verses 22–66).

PARDON AND PEACE

Ideally, from the moment of Baptism, we should live a life of deep faith, centred on the Lord. In practice, we all fall short of that ideal. We fail in our love for God and for others. We close areas of our lives to God's presence, and fail in our vocation to be a living sign of the Good News to the world. Sometimes we can even turn away from the Lord, preferring our own will to his will of love.

All of this is what we mean by sin. It weakens and wounds our friendship with God, but also our bonds with others. It undermines the life and witness of the Church, of which each of us is a vital part.

Rightly we feel ashamed and embarrassed about our sins, especially if asked to admit them openly to another. At the centre of our thoughts should be the amazing richness of the merciful love of God, the Lord who is patient and faithful almost beyond belief. God forgives again and again, and he never refuses to welcome back the sinner who truly returns to him.

There are perhaps two kinds of sinners. Some fail seriously, committing grave sin and deeply wounding their relationships with God and the Church community. Others—and this includes all of us—fail to live up to the ideals of Christian love; this sinfulness is less harmful, but still hinders our openness to the presence of God.

To all sinners, the Lord reaches out as the Good Shepherd in the Sacrament of Reconciliation or Penance (often still called 'Confession'). Through the priest, the Lord himself grants his forgiveness and renews his transforming love within us.

After grave sin, or a period of spiritual apathy, the sacrament involves full reconciliation, a turning back to the Lord, a fresh start, a new beginning. It is almost like a second Baptism. For others, it involves weakening the hold of sinfulness, healing the wounds sin leaves, and growing in holiness.

There are other ways of receiving God's pardon, but this sacrament is the Lord's truly human way of carrying out his divine work of forgiveness.

Three things are expected of the sinner. Firstly, real sorrow for sin, including a change of heart and a determination to try to turn away from sinfulness. Secondly, a humble and open confession of sinfulness to the priest (he can never tell anyone about our sins, and far from thinking less of us as we reveal our failings, he will rejoice at our turning back to the Lord). Thirdly, a willingness to do penance to show our change of heart and repair some of the damage done by our sin. Then the priest, as sacramental representative of the Lord, says the words of absolution (which means 'setting free'): 'I absolve you from your sins in the name of the Father and of the Son and of the Holy Spirit.'

Sinfulness is never a private affair between us and God, but something which weakens the Church. As a sinner I need to be reconciled to the Church as Christ's Body, and so with Christ himself. It is a sacrament we must receive after grave sin, and one we should all celebrate frequently as we continue our pilgrim journey.

Coming to this sacrament is never easy, but it is a marvellous way of receiving the healing pardon, the forgiving welcome, of our Shepherd Lord, who breaks the bonds of our sinful past and sets us free to grow closer to him and to live more fully the life of love. We know that Jesus says to the priest, as he said to the apostles in another context, 'Those sins you forgive, they are forgiven' (John 20:23).

Penance is an important part of the whole pilgrim life of the Christian. It shows our sorrow, our readiness to undo the damage caused by our sin, and our union with Christ in his suffering. Friday is a special day when we remember the first Good Friday by some kind of self-denial, prayer or act of loving kindness.

We need the support of the whole Church in our life of penance. The idea behind indulgences is that as we take on a certain prayer or action, the Church shoulders some of our burden, rather like Simon of Cyrene helping Jesus to carry his cross.

ANOINTING OF THE SICK

Jesus healed the sick, and gave power to his apostles to do the same, anointing the sick with oil (Mark 6:13). St James tells us that if someone is ill, the leaders should anoint and pray over the person (James 5:14–15). These are the roots of the sacrament of anointing the sick. In the past we rather lost the idea of this as a sacrament of healing, calling it instead an 'Extreme Unction' for those near to death. Now we have restored its original understanding as a sacrament of healing for the whole person.

It is a sacrament of deep healing for someone who is really ill. Serious sickness often challenges our faith in a loving God, undermines our service of the Lord and weakens our bonds with the Christian community. This anointing is the Lord's sacramental way of touching the sick person to bring healing where it is most needed. It may well be the restoration of bodily health. It may be an inner healing, a deep peace within, or the strength to cope with suffering while still full of faith. Or it may be the final healing of death, when the Lord takes us to himself and heals in a way far more wonderful than anything which can happen on earth: we are made truly whole! Jesus brings healing by strengthening and renewing the sick person's bonds with his Body, the Church.

Jesus can and does heal today, and there is no wound or brokenness which is beyond his healing power. He will use each of us as instruments of his healing touch, while bestowing special gifts on some as a service to the many (I Corinthians 12:9).

CHRISTIAN MARRIAGE

The whole Christian faith is about love in the richest meaning of the word, involving the real giving and sharing of oneself in selfless sacrifice. God is such love in its fullness, and the source of all real love. He seeks to draw humanity together into a deep unity within his own life. He does this in many ways, but human friendship, affection and love are his most 'natural' human way of doing so. God makes holy all that is truly human, including all true forms of love.

Friendship is a gift from God, a blessing to be cherished (Ecclesiasticus 6:14–17). Deep spiritual friendship between Christians can be a great support in their life as disciples, especially if they pray and worship together.

The intimate friendship of a man and woman in love is also something rooted in God and blessed by him. The Scriptures often compare God's relationship with us to the love between bridegroom and bride, husband and wife. All real love is about self-giving, and the special bond of marriage involves two people giving themselves totally to each other until they are parted by death.

Christian marriage is not just an agreement to live together as husband and wife. It is a vocation, a calling from God to a special–'two-some'–kind of discipleship. Their union is a sacrament, a living symbol of the holy wedding or 'covenant' of God with us, his Bride. The married couple in their joyful life of mutual love are meant to be the Good News come alive, a kind of visual aid of the intimacy God longs for with us (Ephesians 5:25–33). The Lord will use their love as an instrument to others of his own loving presence.

Christian marriage is no easy calling. It is a Gospel commitment, and like any form of discipleship it is a tough, demanding vocation which involves renouncing oneself and taking up the cross of Christ. It is also a calling filled with the joy of Easter.

Marriage involves the totally free, unreserved, unconditional giving of two people to each other. It is founded not just upon mutual feelings, but upon a promise of commitment. It is God who joins together their lives. Because their union is a sacrament of God's faithful and never-ending love, any real marriage is permanent, even if one partner is unfaithful, just as the Lord remains totally faithful to us even if we turn our back on him. Jesus himself said, 'What God has joined together, let no person put asunder' (Matthew 19:6). There can be no divorce when a marriage is truly sacramental and consummated. Christian marriage is for life, till death us do part.

There are couples who are not really married in the first place, perhaps because they were not seriously committing themselves on their wedding day to all that Christian marriage involves, or because they were personally incapable of giving themselves totally to each other with the degree of commitment required. In such cases, the Church can declare that no marriage actually existed at all (an 'annulment'). This is not the same as divorce, which is the putting asunder of two people who are truly married.

Marriage is a complete giving of two people to each other, a commitment to be totally faithful. This obviously includes sexual faithfulness. Adultery is a very grave failure to live the meaning of marriage, striking deep at God's work of 'at-one-ment'.

This especially intimate unity, which only comes about on the wedding day when the couple give themselves totally to each other in a new way, is wonderfully expressed and deepened in the union of bodies involved in God's holy gift of sexual intercourse. Bride and groom leave their parents, and become one flesh: 'They are no longer two, therefore, but one body' (Matthew 19:5). This is why sexual intercourse outside of marriage is a serious misuse of God's great gift. It is only when a couple have reached the stage of final, no-turning-back commitment in marriage that sexual intercourse becomes the God-filled joy it is meant to be. The complete bodily union of husband and wife is the final sealing of the weaving together of their lives, the supreme physical expression of the deep and total love between them.

God's creative work flows from uniting what he has already created. He brings forth new human life through the loving union of two of his beloved creatures. Permanently to refuse to allow God to work through their union is to shut their life to his creative love. Marriage involves a couple being responsibly but unselfishly open to God's own life-making work through their love-making.

Christian marriage is a call to serve together within the Church, not just a personal agreement between a couple. A Catholic therefore must be married in the presence of the Catholic community, in a Catholic church, unless the Bishop gives permission to do otherwise.

ORDINATION TO THE PRIESTHOOD

Christians live their faith in a local church with Christ as their leader and 'overseer' (1 Peter 2:25). We are a people intimately 'at one' with Christ, a royal, priestly and prophetic community anointed with the Spirit to be the Lord's instrument in the world. The risen Jesus is Servant Lord of the Church, and lives among us as our one and only Good Shepherd and High Priest, the Head of his Body, gathering us together, feeding and guiding us, bringing us back when we stray.

How does the Lord make his invisible leadership visibly present and effective? He works in many ways, using the gifts of different people to care, teach and lead, but it is above all through those set aside by the sacrament of ordination that Jesus exercises his role as our Shepherd and Leader.

The priest is the personal living sign in the midst of his pilgrim community that the Lord is there as our High Priest offering himself to the Father, our Head uniting his Body with himself in his sacrifice, our Shepherd nourishing his flock with the gift of himself and gathering them together as one. The priest is not someone 'between' Christ and his people; he makes Christ present, 're-presenting' him, specifically in his pastoral leadership of his disciples.

The priest presides at the Eucharist, absolves sinners, anoints the sick, proclaims and explains the Scriptures with authority, blesses the people and generally leads the whole faith-life of his community. He does these things because of what he became at his ordination, the living sign and instrument, the living icon, the 'walking sacrament' of Jesus as he continues his own ministry among us. Jesus leads the Church through the visible service of his priests.

The priest serves as one of the people, yet one set apart. His vocation enables every member of the Church to live his or her own vocation to the full. The priest is a visible centre of unity, and has the task of helping people to discover and use their gifts in the service of Christ, so that the Church can be what it is called to be, the living sign and instrument of Christ in the world. The priest is essential for the full life of the Church. There is a real need for more people to offer themselves for this vital ministry of pastoral leadership in the name of the Lord.

BE HOLY

Every Christian is called to perfect holiness. To be holy means to share the life of the Holy One, and to live to the full our love for God and each other.

Some Christians are called to give special witness to what perfect holiness and discipleship really involve. Married couples do this by their mutual and selfless love. Others bear witness by living as members of special communities (religious sisters or brothers, monks and friars); by living in a radical way the Gospel ideals of poverty, chastity and obedience, they remind us that there is something—or Someone—infinitely more important than even the greatest joys and blessings of life, including possessions, marriage, sex, family life, and freedom to plan one's own future. By their undivided attention to the Lord, they bear witness to the heart of the Gospel: that the Lord alone must be the centre of our life. The prayer-life of these communities is especially important: they are spiritual 'powerhouses' in the midst of the Church and the world.

ETERNAL LIFE

Death is the event we fear most, yet far from being the end of life, it is the gateway to eternal life and happiness with Christ, deep in God's inner life of love. This is what we mean by heaven. Because salvation is about God drawing us together into his life, heaven will be a family affair where we are fully 'at one' with one another in God.

Heaven is not forced on us, because love cannot be forced, and we are free to say a total 'No' to all God freely offers us. God never stops loving us, but we can shut ourselves in so much that we begin to live a godless hell here and now. Death cements our choice, and God respects our decision. In that sense, those who go to hell (if there are any) put themselves there by refusing God's heavenly gift of himself.

Catholics pray for the dead, rather than just remember them with thanksgiving and hope. We on earth are closely united with those who die, and our prayerful union with them can help their final movement towards God as he leads them deeper into his life.

Some people reach death unready for the fullness of life with God. They have not rejected God, but need God's power to open them up to him. They are purified by the refining fire of the God's Spirit of love, and emptied of all that blocks or hinders God's gift of himself. This is the process which Catholics call purgatory. Because God longs for us to live deep in his presence, he freely reaches out to us at death to make us more able than we can ever deserve to share the wonders of his life.

Heaven will be a glorified life as fully human beings, both 'spiritual' and 'material', body as well as soul. We believe in the resurrection of the body. How this will happen and what we will be like is a total mystery, except that the crucified Jesus has gone before us (I Corinthians 15:35–36).

We are called to be God's holy ones, a communion of saints here and now, and we are united with those disciples already deep in God, in heaven. The saints are our living brothers and sisters in the faith, examples of Christian life and people who pray for us. If we really believe they are truly alive in God, what difference is there between the near 'veneration' given to popular modern Christian figures and that given to the saints in heaven? What difference is there between asking each other to pray for us, and asking the saints to do so, except that they are nearer to God?

MARY, MOTHER OF THE LORD

If what we have said about the saints makes sense, a special devotion to Mary is something very natural. She is the human being with the unique calling from God to be mother of his Son. It was through her that God's Son came into the world as one of us, and she is still his mother today. A deep love for Mary seems to go along with a deep love and worship of her divine Son, and is surely something of which the Lord himself would approve.

Because of her vocation, Mary was kept free from sin from the first moment of her existence: this is what we mean by her immaculate conception. Mary still needed salvation by her Son, but she was saved in the unique way of being preserved from falling by God's grace, rather than being rescued as we are from the pit of human sinfulness.

Mary has been seen as virgin mother from the beginning of the Church. Jesus was conceived in her without the involvement of a human father, without sexual intercourse, and Mary remained a virgin throughout her life of total obedience to God. Like the first creation, the new creation begun in Jesus is entirely God's work. Jesus is literally a 'Godsend'.

Mary is rightly called mother of God or 'God-bearer'. Obviously she is in no way the source of Jesus' divinity, but she was the human mother of God the Son come in the flesh. Calling Mary 'Mother of God' affirms our belief about who her Son really is!

Because of her unique role in bearing Christ to the world, God welcomed her fully into his presence at the end of her life. Instead of suffering bodily corruption, she was taken body and soul to share the risen life of her Son. This bodily assumption into heaven reminds us that God loves and saves the whole human person, body as well as soul.

Mary rejoiced in the God who had done such great things in her, and humbly realized that 'from this day forward all generations will call me blessed' (Luke 1:48). In their special love for Mary, Catholics are simply responding in faith to God's own grace at work in her.

Mary is the great woman of faith, the true disciple, the person strong enough to be God's servant and to let God's will be done in her. She sums up the faithful discipleship to which each of us is called, and embodies in herself the vocation and destiny of the Church. Our great call, as individuals and above all as the communion of the Church, is to be a Christ-bearer, so open to the Lord's presence that we bring him to others by our life of faithful love.

We can do this because of the Lord's own promise to us: 'Know that I am with you always; yes, to the end of time' (Matthew 28:20).

INDEX